The Williams Family

Presents

A Letter to other Trauma Victims

By: K.Moore

Dedication

This heartfelt letter is to everyone who feels alone after enduring any form of trauma. Zeek and Kahlani understand how you feel and are here to offer some comforting words of encouragement. You are not alone enduring the trials of life without a listening ear close by.

1

Zeek's letter of Tragedy

Dear Readers,

I Ezekiel Roger Williams is here to share my story with you.
I like many of you have been the victim of child sexual
abuse at the hands of someone close to me. Being that my
abuser was my father makes this hard for me to even
accept. Watching the way that man would beat my mother
and force her to take drugs was heartbreaking. As a baby

and as a toddler I would cry for my mother when my fathe
was violating my genitals.

Through the tears my heart broke even more to see my
dads friends sexually assaulting my mom. But she was too
high to know what was happening to her at the time. The
moment my mom took me over Mrs. Wilson was the best
moment of my life. But tragedy struck again watching my
mom leave me there. I thought we were going to stay there
together and be safe. My mom Janette promised to come
back for me once she got clean.

That was the longest 6 yrs of my life but also the scariest
when my dad noticed we were gone. When he found me I
thought I was going to die that night. I don't know who
called the cops but I am eternally grateful. For those of you
who read the first book in this series you already know the
condition my body was in at the age of 2 going on 3.

Mrs. Wilson was a lifesaver for me in so many ways , I promise you there is someone out there who will rescue you as well.

While I was composing this letter I thought about all the positive things Mrs.Wilson instilled in me. I want to share with you guys the same encouragement that helped me. I'll go more in depth later on in the letter so be patient with me. It's hard for me going back down memory lane and feeling like my past has me in a chokehold. I know you feel like that right now as you're reading this letter.

Like I told my son Christian's mother Crystal(deceased) Officer Williams to the rescue. I may not be a licensed therapist like Dr. Matthews but I'll try to help you any way I can. Crystal's case, like most of you out there, is uncomfortable to think about or speak about. Going away to College should be an exciting experience for anyone. Yet it was a scary outcome for Crystal.

After being held hostage and raped and beaten for nearly 3 yrs had to be hard for her. For her family it had to be hard not knowing if she was alive or dead all those years. After finding out she was pregnant with my son, I tried to find her family. They were so glad to find her but saddened by her story of what happened to her. They thanked me for getting her a job and finding out we were expecting Christian.

After we buried Crystal and I met my lovely wife Kahlani was the start of a bond I can't even explain. That woman like Mrs.Wilson was a breath of fresh air in my life. She'll talk to you guys later, right now she's at cheer practice with Camille and Ann Marie. I'm going to get some food right now but I'll talk more with you guys in the next letter.

Sincerely:

Officer Williams

2

The Brighter side of Life

Dear Readers

I'm back and ready to brighten your day with some inspiration. For those who are mentally and physically drained from your trauma, this letter is for you. Once you surround yourself with people who will not judge you. When I became a father at the age of 17 I expected people to judge me. With people like my mom and Mrs.Wilson in my corner I had the strength to be a better father to my son than my father was to me.

Don't think it was easy for me to build this strong team around me because it wasn't. The mothers of my 3 oldest children shattered my spirit telling me they didn't want the children we made. I really felt like a failure with all this responsibility on my shoulders. It was hard to not give up after seeing them walk away from my babies. As a man you can imagine how hard it was for me to tell my kids why there was no mommy at our house.

The day I met my wife was a new beginning for me and my small family. We had instant chemistry and a bond nobody ever expected. Finding out that we were both abused by my father made it my mission to be a better man than the one I was named after. Now that I have 3 more children to care for along with my wife I'm feeling better than ever. I'm glad Chief Marshall recommended Dr.Matthews to me.

Going to therapy was great for helping me grow as a man, father and husband. For those who have read "Turning a new Leaf" you see that we have family group therapy. We've even gotten our friends to go through with having therapy to build them up. As long as you are in the company of those who have your best interest at heart you'll be fine. Talking to those who will not pass judgment on your story will make it so much easier.

Don't be afraid to be in a group setting and hearing the stories of others. Sometimes hearing the stories of others relatable tragedies can make your story easier to talk about. Never think that your trauma is any worse than anyone else's because it's just as bad. So many are still running from their trauma like my wife was until we met.

It can feel like a bad horror movie in slow motion when your fear paralyzes you to the point where you contemplate suicide. Please try to follow the path we've taken to get better. My wife will tell you her story later on and she'll go into more detail of what it was like for her. I'm going to hang out with my little ones for a while. I'll talk to you guys about my spiritual transformation after trauma.

If you want you can reread these letters in the meantime while I work on the next letter. When you get my next letter please have your bible next to you. We're going to have service through written letters. I promise you will be so much better by the time you finish reading my letter.

Sincerely,

Officer Williams

3

Spiritual enlightenment

Dear Readers,

Like I said before we're going to have a spiritual growth taking place in this letter. The first step in the healing process is accepting Christ in your life. Let's open our bibles to **1 tim 1:15** which is the beginning to our recovery. I had accepted Christ as a child when Mrs.Wilson read the bible to me. I didn't understand what she was reading at the time. I didn't have a full understanding until I met my wife and went to a bible study with her congregation.

The first thing we talked about in bible study was **Forgiveness**. In **Romans 3:25** where we learn that " God in his forbearance was forgiving the sins that occurred in the past". Just know you're forgiving the perpetrator of your trauma just as God did. It's no judgment passed against you at all for making the courageous step to overcome your past.

Next you should have a healthy routine of prayer and bible reading. Those are things that Mrs. Wilson instilled in me as a child. I went through that routine with my children up until the moment I met my wife. When we included her into the routine with her knowledge of the bible my family was complete. Kahlani told us we needed to set boundaries against our trauma. That leads us to **Isaiah 60:18** where God promises to rid your world of the violence and only salvation will remain.

The next thing to do is identify the places and things that trigger you. Don't go to places that remind you of your trauma unless you feel safe. If certain activities make you dwell on your trauma, respectfully decline your participation. No one should judge you for that; it's part of who you are.

One other thing I chose to do was **Self-Compassion**=the ability to treat myself the same way I would treat my family and friends. It's just like in **1 Peter 3:8** where we are to show " brotherly affection, tender compassion and humility". Then I had to accept my feelings about what happened to me. I had to let go of all the self hate and judgment I held based on me carrying the same name as the man that tortured me as a child.

Sincerely,

Officer Williams

4

More Coping Advice

Dear Readers

Another way I was able to overcome my trauma was to be in the good company of others. Don't be around people who are associates of your abuser. Any person, place or activity that leads you to think or act negatively is unwanted. That's one of the things I love about the relationship I have with my wife and friends. Our date nights are filled with people, places and activities that fill me with pride.

Now that 2 of my children are married and 1 is engaged we can hangout as a group. Even when we get together during the holiday season it's the most relaxing time. For me the most relaxation I get now is with Camille, Brandon & Ann Marie. Also being with my grandbabies Marquis and Heaven takes my mind off of things of the past. I hope my wife feels the same way when she talks to you guys.

My boys Max and Rashad are another piece of my recovery from my past. We always have good times together anytime we are around each other. Even at the station those two keep me laughing. We still reminisce about those bad dates Captain sent us on in the beginning of our career. I feel bad for my boys after knowing their dates have been stalking them. I'm still shocked that those girls showed up on my boys' honeymoons.

And the fact that those crazy women tried to kill my wife's friends. I truly think that was traumatic for my boys the whole time they were on their honeymoons. As men, husbands and fathers we've made it our mission in life to protect our families. We also took a solemn oath to protect our community from people who inflict trauma upon others.

I'll share another thing the guys and I like to do which is team building exercises. We go to places that help build self confidence and trust in oneself. Every week we all get together at one of our houses to play board games or puzzles. Most of the time our kids want to help us cheat which makes it a pretty hilarious night. We also have group dates with our wives which you will learn more about in 4 seasons of Love.

My favorite team building activity with the guys is played in the station. Max came up with it while we were trying to solve a case. The game is called **"Classify This"** . It's a great brain teaser. We use it to sift through the evidence until we find common factors leading us to our perpetrator. We also play **"Salt & Pepper"** at the house with our wives. We mostly like this activity right before we have our couples cooking class.

It's played by each couple choosing 2 items that work well together like (cereal and milk). Tape the name of the item of their choice on their back. Each Of you gets to ask 5 questions to get your partner to guess what is taped on the others back. We also play team building games with the little ones when their friends come over.

It was fun to share my therapy exercises with all of you in the world. I hope you try some of these activities to rise above your trauma. I'm going to stop here for now since Camille is with her friends Cheerleading and it is my day to pick her up. Plus Brandon and Ann Marie want my attention as well. I'll talk to you guys later and give you some more reasons to smile like I do.

Sincerely,

Officer Williams

5

New Beginning

Dear Readers,

In this final letter for this week I want to talk about new beginnings which is the conclusion to dealing with trauma. For me my new beginning was meeting my wife because we shared a trauma bond with the man that abused us. I guess for us knowing that there was another person who understood the situation made it more comfortable to open up.

Seeing our mothers become fast friends after sharing their trauma with one another. That made me proud. I don't know about my wife. You'll have to wait for her response in her letters. We have open-minded conversations with our children everyday. There isn't a topic off limits for us to talk about especially when it comes to school or work. Nowadays there's still hate being spread in the world which isn't even necessary.

I'm trying to be like Christ and love others as Christ loved with an open heart. We teach our children to do the same when they interact with others. No matter how judgmental others may be of your situation, don't allow them to beat you down for what was beyond your control. Even those who choose to be bullies are dealing with some form of trauma. They're just masking their pain by traumatizing others around them.

Let's start encouraging positive behavior to make the world a better place. With that being said I'm going to close out this conversation with a prayer for all of you in the relatable fiction world.

Dear Heavenly father,

I Ezekiel Roger Williams is humbly coming to you in prayer for my readers. All those who are enduring trauma at this very moment and those who are overcoming their own trauma. Hear their silent cries for help and lead them to others like myself. Grant me the strength to help them to the best of my ability? Give them the strength to throw all of their burdens at your altar when they feel weighed down?

I ask all these things in the name your son Jesus Christ

Amen

Like I've been stating, surround yourselves with positive vibes and that's what you'll get in return. Even if you have to take some of my mother's hilarious advice to have a new start at overcoming trauma, I say go for it. I personally wouldn't take my moms advice on anything because it doesn't match my character. But if you do use my mom's advice hopefully it doesn't land you in jail.

It was a pleasure talking to you guys in this series of letters for a week. I hope you received the courage you need to overcome whatever obstacles are in your life at this time. Don't be afraid to ask for help; you never know how many angels God has sent your way. Well until we read together again I'm going to enjoy my last day at home with my little ones. Then tomorrow it's back to the station to solve crime with my boys Max, Malcolm and Rashad.

Sincerely,

Officer Williams

Message from the Author

Thank You to all of you who have followed both the Leaving Trauma Behind and Bonded by Love Series. This book of letters from my two leading characters is the beginning of the final conclusion of the Zeek and Kahlani story. Their hearts are open to everyone around them, even those who were out to harm them.

Please enjoy the rest of their saga as they continue to help others Leave the trauma behind. I'll stop talking now and let you read Kahlani's letters from her heart to yours.

6

Tragic times end in Tragic measures

Dear Readers,

I am Kahlani Marie Coleman-Williams and I am here to share my story of recovery with you. For those of you who read the 1st book you're aware of my traumatic childhood. I'm sure there are others who can relate to it in some way. As a child you're supposed to feel safe around your parents, not afraid. As you know my husband and I didn't have that in our homes growing up.

No child should be afraid of their parents being in the same room with them. But as we see in society some people shouldn't be allowed to have children let alone be around any. As a parent, safety and wellbeing of your children should be a priority. It was for my mother but she wasn't strong enough to fight my dad or my now deceased father in-law.

That great woman put her life and safety on the line for me but, ultimately I had to fight for myself. I'm not proud of the fact that I took my father's life. How could a man call himself a father and let his friend violate your little girl and you co-sign these behaviors as Love. Enough was enough for me. I wasn't going to let them hurt me or my mom anymore. So yes I shot my father 8 times with a police officer's gun without batting an eye.

I was physically empty at that point and saw no other way out. Yes the police were there but they were moving too slow in my 4 yr old mind. Now I personally don't condone gun violence but if that's the closest weapon to you at the time "use it". I know I may not look as tough as I sound in this letter but for the safety of my family I'll kill somebody. That's my word.

I know those of you who are enduring your own trauma right now are at the same point I was. Don't give up on yourself, keep believing and an outcome will come your way. It may not be the outcome you want but at least the trauma will end. The level of bullying that's taking place in schools and the workplace is another safety concern that leads to tragic outcomes.

For me it was school as you have read and the way people view my back story of trauma. The way Danella and her friends ridicule me for being sexually abused made the anxiety of co-existing in the world hard for me. Being gang raped, beaten and left for dead was a level of trauma none of us should have to live with. The peer pressure of my peers to fit in with the crowd was just as bad.

Not knowing who I could trust was another part of my trauma that I had to work on. Until the night I met my now husband of 5 years I wasn't comfortable around men at all. Now I've learned through therapy to watch my surroundings and make sure I'm with people who make me feel comfortable. I want all of you trauma victims to do the same for your own safety.

Now I'm going to go take a break and hang with the kids while my husband is at the station. Camille is such a big helper when she gets home from school and practice. But right now I got it covered TTYL guys

Sincerely,

Kahlani M Coleman-Williams

7

The New Me

Dear Readers

I'm going to share with you how I discovered my self worth after my trauma. For me it started when I went off to College and had to start adulting. You know (paying rent, bills, buying groceries, buying a car etc). Having 2 internships in the fields that are near and dear to my heart made that work out for me. Even though I'm a teacher now, I still volunteer at the hospital where I did my internship.

I still had nightmares of my childhood and teen years as an adult. But being in the company of Regina during my internship at the elementary school was like medicine. When she referred me to Cora at the middle school was the best gift anyone could've given me. It was then that I met the only man to make me feel safe. But I still don't understand how both of my friends knew so much about my man and couldn't find a man of their own.

I was so glad when Zeek introduced them to Rashad and Max. We started going on group dates and having real fun experiences. Every activity puts a permanent smile on us ladies every weekend. We'll talk more about our group date activities in **"4 Seasons of Love"**. For now let me tell you the other experience that changed me. And that's becoming a parent to 6 wonderful human beings.

After losing 2 babies during my childhood after being raped it was a blessing to meet Malcolm, Harmony and Christian. For them to call me mom was music to my ears and seeing how much they cared for me when I was afraid at times made it easy to choose not to leave this family. When I found out I was pregnant with Camille it was even better.

The kids were just as excited as Zeek and I about the new baby. When she was born they all wanted to be around her more than they wanted to go to school. Once the kidnapping happened Christian and Camille had a bond that can't be compared to anything. Even now that Christian is finishing College and about to get married he still comes by to see about Camille and the twins.

I'm telling you these things as examples of what can help you escape your mental trauma. It may not take place in the same fashion as my life but don't be afraid to experience joyful things. The friends you make down the line can be just the anchor you need to maintain your sanity in this cruel world. Allow my words to be your therapy for your new start in life.

After becoming a mom and a wife I accepted Christ as the head of my life. Learning the bible again after the death of the woman that raised me(Mrs. Johnson)deceased was just wonderful. I truly believe that was what led Zeek and I to finding each other. When he shared with me that Mrs.

Wilson read the bible to him as a child. I felt like I had found my equal.

Sometimes when you get around people of likemindedness you can uplift each other. The things that used to burden you will be a figment of your imagination. Then it will be your turn to inspire someone else. Until I get back with the next letter let my story of courage lead you to overcoming your trauma. See you guys in a little while .

Sincerely,

Kahlani M Coleman-Williams

8

Safe Zone Activities

Dear Readers,

I'm sure my husband told some of the things we do with our friends and family. Sometimes it's just going to the park with the twins or cheer practice with Camille. If you're in a relationship maybe having a date night routine on Friday or Saturday nights. I never knew these types of activities would help with my trauma until I met Zeek.

When he took me on our first date I finally felt free of my fears.

I don't know how he planned that date or if the kids helped him but it was the best date of my life. Now we go on two date nights a week but we'll elaborate more on them in "**4 seasons of Love**". But I can't stress enough how important it is to free yourself of your trauma and fears. My husband told me about his activities at the station with the guys. I decided to tell Cora and Regina about them to see if we could do the same around the school.

We combined our classes together for a field trip to do some team building activities. We took them camping in the mountains for one weekend to practice survival skills. Another weekend we did a photo shoot with the kids at the nature preserve. They loved it and us as teachers made us feel good that they enjoyed themselves. At school I hear the kids telling their peers that we're the greatest teachers ever.

Now that I think about it, those activities made me feel better about myself and my choice to become an educator.

Also me and the girls like to go to karaoke sometimes to practice our vocal skills. Our husbands send us to the salon and spa 1 time a month so they can hang with our children. We do the same for our husbands but they won't go to the spa without us. Max and Rashad think all the workers at the spa are conspiring to get them to cheat. I think they're being dramatic but you know they take relationship advice from my mother in-law.

Since we're all still happily married I guess Janette gives some useful advice . Even though most of the things Janette tells people to do are things only she can get away with. The rest of us would be in jail for trying to act like Janette in any moment of crisis in our relationship. Nonetheless Janette is the most entertaining one out of the family. When we have our group dates she never fails to make us laugh. Yet she's the only one who doesn't think anything is funny.

I realized that what I needed in life was someone with a sense of humor about everything. As you may have read in previous books Janette has beef with any and every one she feels is trying to steal our husbands. Pop was right they should've had her on the force to interrogate every suspect of a crime. It is a little awkward and hilarious to see her argue with the waitresses at restaurants about flirting with our husbands at the table.

It's nothing wrong with a little bit of comedy in the circle but someone like Janette can be sidesplitting. I love my mother in-law for finding a comedic way to deal with her trauma. It's hard to believe that Zeek is her son because he's so serious when he deals with people outside of our circle. He only clowns around at home with us or at the station with the guys.

As you've seen in prior stories we as a family of friends do a lot of team building activities to maintain a sense of normalcy in our lives. My hubby told me he let you guys know about our couples cooking with my mom and dad. That is the best stress reliever ever, especially for a person like me who likes to try new things.

I also enjoy seeing my kids in the kitchen with my dad full of smiles. If you have kids taking part in an activity that they like could also be healing for you. The bond you have with your children or the children in your community can help them overcome any trauma they may be enduring. Being a community volunteer can speak volumes for you and the impact you make on others.

Well I'm going to call it a day with this letter to you guys and go take a nap. Since the twins are taking a nap also maybe I can get 30 mins before they get up. So be good to yourselves and those near and dear to your hearts. We'll talk more tomorrow and I hope to inspire you with more encouraging words.

Go have a hearty meal and a hug from those around you before calling it a night. On behalf of the Williams family, have a good night and sweet dreams.

Sincerely,

Kahlani M Coleman-Williams

9

A Spiritual Calling

Dear Readers,

Now that we've overcome our trauma in the last letter, let's go into another topic that helped my family. I know my husband was happy to find out that I knew a lot about the bible. When we started dating he would call me before he went to bed. We'd read a scripture and I'd explain it to him and I could hear the amazement in his voice through the phone. Then we'd pray before hanging up for the night.

Y'all that man still doesn't know how much that prayer helped me sleep at night.

The power of prayer is strong in our hearts which led us to sharing it with our friends. Max started saying that Zeek and I were the marriage counselors of our generation. I tell everyone I meet that it was the christian upbringing I had that made my words so gracious and seasoned with salt. As a family we have family worship every Wednesday night with our kids. Zeek and I believe that it's our right as citizens to lift up every person around us.

This is an example of how being leaders makes it easier to overcome any obstacle. By doing this you are being like Christ and making new disciples. When others look up to you as a role model that will make the trauma less of a burden on you. Be good to others even if they aren't good to you. The more good you do for others the more blessings will come your way.

Now let's take a look at **1 Thess 5:14** where we are told to " speak consolingly to those who are depressed, support the weak and be patient toward all". This is the godly way I was raised to live after all of my childhood trauma. I had to explain it to my husband so he could stop harboring so much hate towards his father. I had to show him how this scripture was the inspiration behind our choices in careers.

The way I speak to my students and the way he deals with suspects shows in this scripture. This scripture also applies to how we deal with our children. Even when we see our friends are feeling down we turn to **Proverbs 27:9** which speaks of "sweet friendship springing from sincere counsel". That's all we want is to see those around us be uplifted and filled with the christian qualities of God.

Even though the people who harmed us are deceased now we still pray for their souls to rest peacefully. As well as the people who have harmed our children are prayed for everyday. In doing this we live by the words at **Romans 8:17** being children of god and joint heirs with Christ.

As I close out this letter I hope you feel better about dealing with your trauma. And I hope you feel inspired enough to go help others. I know I do feel less burdened by my memories of my childhood. The bond I have with my family and friends is just as strong as my bond with Christ. I hope yours is as well everytime you pick up your bible or one of K.Moore's books to read.

For now I'm going to go make dinner for the family and get the twins ready for their bath. Have a good night everyone in reading land. I'll see you next time. Have a safe and blessed day from my family to yours. We love all of you from the bottom of our hearts. Hug all those around

youI'm sure they could use a hug as much you do at this

moment.

Sincerely,

Kahlani M Coleman-Williams

10

Moving on strong

Dear Readers,

In the end you have to take ownership of your life after the trauma. Accepting that the past happened and now it's time to move on. In the first book K.Moore told us not to spend the rest of our lives being held captive by our fears. I took that message to heart and applied it to everyday life. I told my children everyday while they were in school and now I tell Camille and the twins the same thing.

Everyday that I spend with those close to me is filled with fun in a judgment free zone. Seeing all of my friends and family laughing and having a good time makes me realize how fortunate I am. Even me writing these letters to you guys is helping me move forward with my life. I'll ask Zeek later if writing his letters was therapeutic for him in Leaving his Trauma Behind.

At school I tell my students to keep a journal of their feelings and thoughts. Then we have group discussions as a class to help uplift one another. I'm so proud of how much my students have opened up since writing. Just last week a couple of my students informed me that they want to become writers in the future. As their teacher I look forward to reading their work in the future.

Sometimes when I'm alone like now I do some journaling myself. I sit in bed and talk to Zeek about how I'm feeling through my writings. We identify my triggers and try to come up with ways to deal with them. That man is the best friend I've ever had when times get rough. Together we practice letting go of old (bad) memories to make room for the present and future memories.

I get with the girls for a bit of self care once a week to destress. We go to the gym for two hours one week. Then we'll go to the nail salon or get our hair done at each other's homes. It's the best time spent with people who love me without judgment. I know Zeek goes to the barber shop with the guys. They go play golf in the spring and summer time. But the one thing they love to do the most is spend time with their kids. That makes us ladies so happy to see them with their children full of smiles.

If these types of activities aren't helping you try finding a support group. Your local hospital or community center has resources to keep you safe. There is always someone willing to listen to you so you don't feel alone in the world. I never want to see my fellow man stuck in a space that isn't comfortable for them to live in.

Again guys believe me I've been at that low point just as some of you are at now. I know I keep repeating myself but it's a must invest in yourself before someone else can invest in you. Build yourself up to stand tall against the opposition so others take you seriously. Don't forget my number 1 rule which is to "never spend your life being held captive by your fears".

Here we are at the end of this book of letters finally and I can breathe a sigh of relief. I hope the weight of the world is no longer on your shoulders. Keep building your faith and believing in yourself to overcome your trauma. This letter to you guys reminds me of my favorite Mariah Carey song "Anytime you need a friend". Don't ever feel lonely because there's always a shoulder for you to lean on. Now that I think about it I'm going to listen to that song while I make dinner tonight.

Good night to all of you readers in the relatable fiction world. Zeek and I will be going to hang out with our 3 babies for the rest of the weekend. Because on Monday it's back to work for me and another day of work for Zeek. This has been a very relaxing and therapeutic week's vacation for me. Inspiring you guys to feel better about yourselves makes me feel better.

I love all of you for following the lives of the Williams family. We along with our friends can't wait to entertain you in the next 5 books to conclude the series.

Yours Truly,

Kahlani M Coleman-Williams

11

Final Testimonies

Zeek- As a young man it was hard to understand why my parent would hurt me. It wasn't until I was placed in the care of Mrs. Wilson and she explained to me that it was the devil controlling my father. Even though I don't think that's entirely true I do believe my father was under the influence of something. Maybe it was a demonic possession or drugs or a combination of both.

I think my trauma is what led me to choose Law Enforcement as my career of choice. I did and do want to protect the innocent like myself who were defenceless against those we were supposed to trust. When a child is brought into the world they deserve love not hate from their parents. The world we're brought up in is cruel enough.

I learned from Dr. Matthews that some predators are just a product of their environment. Maybe that was the case with my dad. Possibly my grandparents did the same things to him that he did to me. I don't know any of the members of my dads family but after finding Destiny's family for Harmony I'll ask Max to help me find mine. Come to think of it, I've never met anyone in my moms family either.

Janette has a lot of explaining to do about that because my kids need to know their family. I'm sure it's the back of their minds, especially Christian as he's about to become a married man soon. I want to do everything I can to give them the answers they need. These answers will be good for me as well to understand where my parents came from. The only thing is mom might start acting crazy when I ask her questions so I'll let the kids ask her.

Hopefully by the end of the series I'll have the answers to get closure to my trauma. Even after meeting my wife it's been hard for me to keep pretending that I'm okay over the years. I'm sure she's known the whole time because she seems to notice a lot of things about everyone around us. She likes to talk at night when we're alone and the kids are in bed for the night. No matter how much I try to avoid certain topics I hear her out with no interruption. I accept her guidance and fall deeper in love with her every day.

I even listen to my kids when they want to talk no matter what time of the day it is. I know they think I have all the answers but what they don't know is that their mom helps with all those answers. Even when Max and Rashad ask me for advice I go to my wife first before I can answer them. Y'all don't understand how lost I am most of the time when people ask for my opinion.

I'm like a lost puppy when my wife isn't around and I'm so glad God put her in my life. Now I'm officially done testifying about my trauma to you guys. I'm gonna go play with the munchkins in the living room. We'll all see you in the next book for some fun days around and about the great state of Tennessee.

Kahlani- As a little girl it was hard for me to understand why my father didn't protect me. It was even hard to understand why he let his friend harm me the way he did. As an adult, to be stalked by the man who became my father in-law was worse. Not to mention my father in-law was my dads best friend and the perpetrator of my trauma. For a long time I did contemplate ending my life as an escape from it all.

I didn't think men could ever be trusted until I met my husband. Our trauma bond may seem odd to some but knowing we were both abused by the same man brought us closer. I guess we thought we could protect each other from the bad guy in our lives. Then there are days when I think about the fact that my husband is the protector of the people.

As a member of the police force people put their lives in his hands everyday. Don't get me wrong I'm worried about his safety every time he walks out the front door. I never know if there's someone out to harm him or our family. Last time we thought our family was safe a jealous teen girl tried to harm Ann Marie and Camille to win Christian's heart.

People don't have a heart of Love in the world, just plain cruelty. My family is never rude to those around us, yet so many want to bring us harm. Everyone that meets us says that " we are not part of the world" just like Jesus Christ said in the bible. In the same token you as survivors shouldn't concern yourself with the opinions of those who pass judgment against your trauma.

But there are those like my father in-law and my bullies from high school who will laugh at your pain. I had to train myself to be strong in the face of hard times. You may have to build a defence mechanism to endure your trauma but in the end you will be a survivor.

Zeek- My baby is still up here talking to you guys I see. That woman has a heart of gold and I'm so glad God brought us together. Anything she's told you in her letters is inspired by God himself. Even our kids say that she's an angel and I agree with them. Having a family with Kahlani was the best part of my recovery.

She doesn't know it but by the time we get into the next book she might be pregnant again. I know she said she didn't want anymore kids after the twins were born. But I'm gonna keep trying to put as many babies in her as I possibly can. Just wait and see for yourselves in the next book and share in our happiness with our family.

Maybe my boys will have some more kids on the way in the next couple of books. We love these school teachers we married and nothing will ever change that. When you find your equal hold onto them because it's always good to be with someone who makes you better. Now baby, let's stop talking these people's ears off and go be with our family.

Kahlani- I heard what my hubby said and I will be going to play with the kids shortly. As for the other thing he said we'll see about that in the next book. He thinks I was kidding about having my tubes tied after having the twins. I wish our fiends all the best if they're having more kids.

All I'm worried about is getting ready for Christian and Desiree's wedding. I know my son said they would be getting married in 2032 but I don't think that's going to happen. I see the way they look at each other and it reminds me of me and Zeek. Even when they're apart from each other they want to speed that wedding day up. And since they asked for my help with the wedding, we're going to have it sooner than later.

I just hope nothing and no one will try to ruin their wedding. I need to get on the phone with Desiree's mom to start the planning process for the wedding. Maybe I'll ask Bro. Stanford if he'll officiate the wedding for them. I need to spend some time with my new daughter in-law to talk about this Pittsburgh Steelers Wedding.

Zeek- Yeah wife I think you should go over to build a relationship with our daughter in-law. I'll be with Malcolm and Travion talking to Christian. As you guys can see we focus on positive things to overcome our past traumas. I hope you'll join us in the rest of this book series. As you can see we're adding more members to our family.

I pray for all of you to overcome your trauma and live happily like my family. We're officially signing off for now, see you guys later. Peace and Love from the Williams Family to all of you. Thank You again for following my family's story throughout this series. I hope we fill your hearts with joy and inspiration in all of these books.

I can't say it enough, please go support our girl K.Moore in her writing journey. Enjoy the **Leaving Trauma Behind**

and Bonded by Love Series. I see big things happening for k.Moore in the future of her fiction writing style.

Love and Blessings from the Williams Family. Have a good night y'all.

Contact Me

E-Mail: relatablefictionwriting@gmail.com

Instagram: soultavern_owner2020

Facebook: nakeialdavis-moore

Tik Tok: leavingtraumabehind4

X: leavingtrauma4

Author Bio

I am a single mom of 1 with a lot of time on my hands. With a background in Management and Customer Service I was ready for a change after being laid off. After helping my son with a homework assignment I decided to start my writing journey.

It was my son who encouraged me to continue in writing the story of the Williams family. He told me "mom I knew you were a great writer, I was waiting for you to believe in yourself". So thank you Josiah for having faith in your mom.

Insight into the next book

Get ready for some good family and friends spending time together. Forgiveness being given to a former foe. The beginning of a bond between a father and his children. More hilarious stories from Janette that will make you shake your head. A wedding is being planned for Christian and Desiree. And lots of couples activities throughout this **4 Seasons of Love.**

Another message from the Author

All the social issues that are brought to light in each of my series need to be taken seriously. All of our children need to feel safe at all times and no teen or adult should be abused by another person. Let's continue to push forward like Zeek and Kahlani to inspire others to overcome their trauma. Again thank you for your support as I try to lift up my peers and the youth of today. Happy Reading to all of you out there in the world.

K.Moore

Printed by Libri Plureos GmbH in Hamburg,
Germany